Starkweather Dreams
Landscape with Figures

Christopher Conlon

Starkweather Dreams
by Christopher Conlon

ISBN-10 1-894953-57-6
ISBN-13 978-1-894953-57-3

Published in Canada by Creative Guy Publishing
Vancouver, BC Canada
First Printing June 2009

Cover painting: ©Matt Sesow, "Lost in a Daydream"
http://www.sesow.com
sesow@sesow.com

Cover photograph: Library of Congress Archives
No rights warranted or implied.

Acknowledgements

Several of these poems (some under different titles) originally appeared in the journals *Poet Lore* and *Tamaphyr Mountain Poetry,* while others were first published in the anthologies *Poetic Voices Without Borders* and *Poetic Voices Without Borders 2.* Many thanks to the editors of these publications.

Starkweather Dreams
Landscape with Figures

Christopher Conlon

creative guy publishing
vancouver | canada

Contents

Three

for Gary A. Braunbeck

One

Charlie Dream

They's fryin' him tonight   the voice confides
in my dream   *him*   *Starkweather tonight*
(countrified fake   -backwoodsy like hicks
in bad movies)   and I am
in the death chamber   Charlie in the hard
straightbacked electric chair   without
straps   just a kind of
metal bowl atop   his head
to jolt   the juice   in
and he looks   as he looked: (Presley
sideburns   James Dean   windbreaker
Bogart   cigarette   between his fingers)
smaller than I'd   remembered   or imagined
slighter   traces of   baby fat softening
his cheeks   freckles   but the familiar
Brando sneer   molding   his mouth
(voice now   behind my ear   whispering *They's fryin'*
him tonight yeah   *justice comin'*   *hot*
an' hard   *courtesy the state*
of Knee-braska   *in the good ol'*   *U. S. of A.*)
the switch the switch   I know hundreds
of plain folk   outside   would love
to throw   the switch   is in my hand
it looks like   a light switch
in my home   or yours   ten times   bigger
giant ON   painted black just   above it
OFF below   and the room   is

small   close-packed   dark yet
I sense people   all around   murmurings
on every   side and   as I look
toward Charlie   I see
Caril there   in his lap   their arms
around each other   her head leaning   to his
touching it   or rather   the metal   bowl around it
she wears   blue blouse   jeans white   cowboy boots
strictly the   all-American   country girl from
Life   or *Look*   and she sucks greedily
at a half   -empty bottle   of Pepsi
in her child   -sized hand smiling   pleasantly
between swallows   I know I
should throw   the switch shove it
upward watch   them smoke   and shudder
for as I   stand there   in the crowded room
I see   *my brother*   *falling*   in subzero
Nebraska night   his face   burst
in screaming   shotgun fog   without even
a jacket against   December   lunar cold
see   *my daughter*   *falling*   down abandoned
storm cellar   steps   back of her head
splayed open   bright   as sunflowers
feel   the knife   in my own   back my own
belly   my own   chest
my body   raged apart   and see
the two   of them   smiling   goading me
to *do it*   *do it*   switch   in my hand
and I press   on it   push   it up
(it   weighs   hundreds   of   pounds)
and as   I do   the room   suddenly   grows

8

brilliantly!   bright!   hum of!   2200! volts!
sheeting! throughout it!   spitting!
crackling!   the room!   alive! with current!
voices! screaming!   everywhere!   around me!
my own hand   blueglowing   smell of
my flesh   sizzling while   in the chair
Charlie's   metal bowl   becomes a golden
halo the two   of them
embracing   in light   giggling sharing
her Pepsi   between them leaning   together
watching   us   watching   me
enjoying   the show

TWO

Charlie's Vision

Someday will be the perfect day,
a day among dogwoods and fir trees,
sun splashing over his face, far
from school, from brothers
and sisters, from the soiled world
of man: Someday he'll meld
with the Nebraska wilderness, live
among the beasts and birds, listen
to the wind stroking the buffalo grass,
and when he kills, as he must,
after all, to live, to survive,
it will be only for food, and he'll
carefully cradle each fallen squirrel
or rabbit in his arms, letting its blood
soak into his own skin, taking
its unique life-force into himself,
and this is so vivid in his brain,
a world of peace, of nature,
of himself *in* nature, himself *as* nature,
that he'll cry at times, weep like
a woman, reaching in his mind
to this someday-vision hovering like
a northern flicker before him, always
almost within his grasp, always just not.

Memory: Charlie

He woke once to wind, to branches
clacking against the window
like the bones of dead men,
heard cars on the road coming
for him—knew they were coming
for him, to take him away forever,
and he knew then that the world was
wicked, the world was *hateful,* the world
was against him, out to destroy him.

He stayed awake until morning, eyes
wide open, breath shallow and quick,
and he knew he'd beaten them then,
all of them, just as he'd beat them
again and again, just as he'd keep on
beating them, the rest of his beaten life.

Empty Space

Charlie will always be proud
of Guy, his father: roofer, handyman,
shoe repairer, a man who could take a tool
and fix anything with it, a man
who taught him everything there was
to know about cars, dogs, guns, girls.

But his mother, Helen, worndown
waitress, frightens him: broken by life,
he can picture her flying apart, bits of her
soaring disconnected into gray void,
leaving only an empty space behind,
leaving him, an empty space, behind.

Charlie's Death

She comes to him without warning,
sometimes just a mournful whistle
at distance, more often a figure
in his bedroom window, half-woman,
half-animal, no arms, no neck,
no ears, no face, reminding him
his time on God's Earth is rushing
to its close—once taking him
on a journey in a flaming coffin
to a valley where the streets were lined
with fire, the coffin melting away,
leaving him naked, alone, but the flames
were warm, like golden bathwater,
and he bathed in them, bathed and sang,
and that was when he knew that he
loved her, loved Death, and would return,
someday, to her womb of fire.

Caril With an i

After her father left she would drape
her mother's fanciest dress
over her shoulders, spread on
rouge, mascara, lipstick, a flouncy
flower-filled hat, and stand out
in the dirt road facing their house, saying
My name is Caril with an i and my daddy
will be back soon, while winter drained
the Nebraska sky, and darkness rushed in.

Sputnik

Caril and her mother
get along, for a while—
shared chores, TV together
at night, but soon it's
a new stepfather, and she's
shunted aside—a leftover,
she knows, from Mom's
other life, her dad's, hers,

and she has no life, now,
cut loose from the world
like Sputnik, floating
without an earth to pull her
back, to hold her forever.

Slow Learner

Once she stands naked
before her bedroom mirror,
leans close to the glass, studies
her forehead, then slams it
hard with the heel of her hand.
Stupid, stupid, stop being stupid,
she whispers, repeating what
her teacher had said to her that day,
Caril Ann, a year behind
everyone else, math skills bad,
reading skills bad, spelling, everything
bad, just plain, well, *stupid,*
that's all, and she bangs her head
again and again, making it hurt,
trying to dislodge the brains
she feels sure must be in there somewhere,
hits herself until tears of rage fly down
her cheeks, spatter her shoulders
and stomach, hiding the other tears
she'll always refuse to set free, to see.

Memory: Caril

She tries to remember what she remembers
about her father, but finds that she remembers
little: an odor of tobacco, maybe,
a shuffling step, a tilt of the head,
and she tries to remember if he'd
loved her, tries to remember if she remembers
him saying that to her, saying anything
to her, tries to remember what she remembers,
wonders if he ever remembers her, or remembers to.

Escape Route

She knows he wonders
why her grades are so poor,
why she's so slow, and he tries
to help her with homework
sometimes, but she doesn't get it,
and he thinks she's dumb,
she knows, and she is,
dumb as a dishrag, dumb as dirt.

At dinner she tries to think
of funny things to say to him,
but they come out wrong
and he just looks at her,
like Mom, now, just looks at her,
and she doesn't belong there,
she knows, isn't real to them anymore,
dumb as a dishrag, dumb as dirt.

She'll wish at times she could
leave the earth entirely, fly into space
like Sputnik, join another world
like the ones in those sci-fi movies,
Forbidden Planet, say, *Rocketship X-M,*
be queen to millions, but she can't,
she knows, she's just Caril Ann forever,
dumb as a dishrag, dumb, dumb as dirt.

Numbered for the Bottom

He sees, at sixteen, how the world works.
His hands bruised, torn, infected half the time
from the garbage he hauls, chucking great
bins filled with rancid cheese, rotten meat,
paint cans, maggoty rats, his body drenched
in the filth of it, the stench that brands him,
that doesn't go away no matter how he washes
and scrubs. Even if he puts on a jacket and tie,
takes a girl to a nice restaurant with proper silver
and cloth napkins, he knows they're laughing
at him, garbage man in fancy pants, dumb-looking
as a little girl in her mother's cocktail dress.
They had me numbered for the bottom, he'd say
later, even then wondering who did the numbering
in this world, wondering if he could rip away
someone's other, better number, re-number
the entire earth, before his own number was up.

To Him

To him there's nobody cuter, nobody
kinder than Caril: majorette boots,
jeans, men's shirts, ponytail bobbing
in Nebraska wind. At thirteen, fourteen
she's no smarter than him, in fact she's
impressed with him, his car, his money,
his hair: he's no stupid shit garbage man
to her, no backward dropout kid to her,
no squint-peering four-eyes, just Brando,
Dean, Mitchum, a man's man. To him
there's nobody at all like Caril, who sees him
for himself, the first ever to know Charlie
Starkweather, to view him clear, to feel awe.

First Sight

in her eyes
>he's manly

in her eyes
>he's sexy

in her eyes
>he's grownup

in her eyes
>he's dangerous

in her eyes
>she's lost
in his eyes

Loving Charlie

Together in his room,
comic books sprawled
on the floor around them,
Caril, thirteen, would say,
Charlie I love every hair
on your head and to prove it
she'd pluck one—
long, rust-colored, oily—
run it slowly across her lips,
lick it languorously end to end,
swallow it whole.

Garbage Man

They tell her to *stay away from him,*
too old for her, good-for-nothing
garbage man, and she pictures him
covered in garbage, sees herself
licking garbage from his face,
mustard, oil, butter, grease,
eating garbage from his clothes,
old newspapers, hamburger wrappers,
wilted lettuce leaves, bloody Kotexes:
until he's clean again, until they both are,
like snow, like sun, unsoiled, baby-pure.

The Skins of Dead Men

He does what he can to dress
like the man he should be:
but thrift shops don't have atomic-white
form-fitting T-shirts, or bright red
windbreakers with collars
that angle just so, or blue jeans that hug
your groin tight like a woman, so
Charlie's shirts are stained gray
in the armpits, his windbreaker too big
and not red at all, his blue jeans
colorless, too loose, ripped at the crotch
and fixed with heavy black thread
that's slowly unraveling.
In the mirror, without
his glasses, he can convince himself
for a moment of his swaggering cool,
but if he moves at all it's
Stumblebum City, bumping into walls,
knocking over tables, and yet with them on
he sees himself, knows
himself for what he is, cut-rate, fake,
a Salvation Army Dean, and he knows
that the people who'd owned these clothes
would have despised him as everyone
everywhere despises him, and later he'll say
it was *like wearing their skins,* being in
those clothes, *like wearing the skins
of dead men,* and it makes him dead, him,
Charlie Starkweather, doomed from the start
to be dead, to die, to keep on dying.

Charlie's Nature

He would draw a bead on a squirrel
those Sunday mornings in the forest:
have it dead in his sights, but
he didn't like shooting animals, preferred
arrows, knives, their silence,
their stealth and dignity, but *myself
not being an expert* he relied
on the surekilling .22. Still,
sometimes he wouldn't shoot at all,
just watch the animal living in nature,
ponder how he would like to live
in nature, a cabin somewhere, even
an old shack, hunting game, gathering
berries, firewood, and a nice girl to fuck,
Caril maybe, to give him babies,
little Starkweathers to frolic with
on the forest floor, to raise up
right, to teach to hunt, to trap,
catch rain in barrels, to make clothes
from leaves and vines, to catch fish
with their bare hands: to live far
from unnatural cities, unnatural towns,
far from mankind, most unnatural of all.

Theory of Relativity

It's the first one she's ever, at thirteen,
really seen: and though she doesn't
say it, she's horrified at its blue wormlike
veins, its slimy oozing effusions,
its sheer *size:* she can hardly believe
anything like *that* is made to fit
inside a girl, and wonders if Charlie
isn't somehow malformed, mutated.

Later, behind a shelf in Charlie's room,
she finds a magazine—grainy black
and white photos on woodgrain
paper—and she sees that
every man pictured is bigger
than Charlie.

From then she's kind
to him, sympathetic, stroking
and licking it
as he pleases, making him happy
for a moment
or two: gently, lovingly
swallowing his shame.

Little Sister

When her half-sister Betty Jean is brought
home from the hospital, Caril Ann stands
over her crib at night, trying to love her:
squeezes her eyes shut, whispers
I love my sister. I love my sister in moonlight,
yet can't not picture her old lumpish step-
father atop her mother, banging away
like a shotgun inside her, and staring down
at Betty Jean in bluewhite nightglow
Caril Ann feels violated, as if he'd shoved
his cock into *her,* forced *her* to spurt out
this stranger, this thing, this baby,
and she feels she could kill him then,
blast away his goddamn balls…
I love my sister. I love my sister, she thinks,
or tries to, language breaking inside her
as everything, now, is breaking inside her.

"Moody New Star"

Charlie would never forget first seeing
that issue of *Life,* March the seventh,
1955, with its feature on Moody New Star
James Dean—he had only one movie
out, which Charlie hadn't gone to, but that *face:*
tousled hair, arched eyebrows, hurtpuppy eyes—
the photos taken on Dean's trip home

to Fairmont, Indiana, the streets and barns
so like those of Lincoln, Nebraska,
and one photo especially, that Charlie cut out
and slid into his wallet: Dean
at Hunt's General Store, it said,
on Main Street, sitting up in a casket, hands
folded, eyes piercing straight into

your soul, saying clearer than words,
You put me here   you caused my torment
look! dead   before my time—and after
Dean did die, Charlie knew the actor's
one mistake: he only succeeded   in the world,
didn't take revenge on it   for his pain,
didn't shred it   in his jaws

didn't rip it apart   with his bare hands

Bloodrush

Charlie won't remember,
later—:

when it was that his dark
dreams—:

became luminous waking
visions—:

when it happened that his idle
fantasies—:

of shooting Mrs. Mott, his
teacher—:

or Marky Bliss, the grinning
bully—:

went from movieland in his
head—:

to something that he might
do—:

do really, in the world, the real
world—:

or what they thought of as
real—:

but from then he was high
explosives—:

ready to blow, his eyes dark
crosshairs—:

and it was power, bloodrush,
joy—:

knowing he was the bringer of
darkness—:

knowing they were, all of them,
doomed—:

Love: Caril

When they would lie together in tall grass
hearing wind overhead and owls,
his fingers roaming her face, her hands stroking
his hair, it was as if their four eyes
were two, their two minds one—

and she knew he was thinking, they both were
thinking, of that movie, James Dean
and Natalie Wood in the abandoned house:
I love somebody, and it's so easy…
Why is it easy now? And she knew

that nobody had ever felt this way before,
such warmth, such peace, a new world
undreamed, unimagined, yet so easy,
and anyone who tried to enter it, she knew,
would be pushed out, rejected, might even

have to die, like Sal Mineo in that movie.

Love: Charlie

Before Caril he dreamed of killing *for no reason,*
but then with her eyes, her voice, her   soft fingers,

he'd *found a reason, something*   *worth killing for,*
and it was a tribute to her,   an honor bestowed:

he would remake the world   for her,
burn the fucker down, build it up again   in Their image

Victim: Robert Colvert

Are you warm enough? his wife asked him
on the phone—graveyard shift, Crest gas station
out on Cornhusker Highway—and, later, more
than the murder itself, maybe, more than the fact
that Bob Colvert was only twenty-one, his wife
with a baby on the way, the town would talk
of him being driven out past the railroad tracks,
six below, wind, and when Charlie burst open
his head and chest with the twelve-gauge, left
his blood rivered and freezing in the frozen dirt,
Bob had on only coveralls, no jacket, no gloves,
and the town wondered what kind of a person—
was it even a person?—would do such a thing, not
the killing, just a middle of the night robbery
gone bad, maybe, but not allowing Bob his jacket—
fleece-lined, hanging right there on the hook
inside the station—in that cold, no comfort at all
in that awful December night, and that
was when the town first knew fear, knew
something was loose in their land,
something terrible, something terribly cold.

Charlie's Version, Caril's

924 Belmont Avenue: Caril's there, or isn't, when the fight begins, when her stepfather, Marion Bartlett, shouts at him to *get the hell out of this house, leave them alone, leave Caril alone,* she's there, or isn't, when her mother Velda screams *She's pregnant isn't she isn't she!* and slaps at his face, there, or isn't, as Charlie grabs the rifle leaning against the wall and fires, the sound much smaller than anyone might have thought, like firecrackers, slamming Marion back up against the door as if he'd been plowed over by a hurricane, dropping heavily, instantly a carcass, and then again, Velda staggering toward Betty Jean in the crib, there, or isn't, when the screaming starts, Velda's or Betty Jean's or her own, there, or isn't, when her mother lurches down to the floor, jerks and flinches

as if with hiccups then lies still forever, there, or isn't, when Charlie turns the butt of the rifle toward her sister, brings it down with a grunt, *thwack, thwack,* there, or isn't, to hear the silence then, to feel the stillness in the deep winter air, there, or isn't, to look away toward the television, toward the cold street, and she sees none of it, coming home from school, or sees all of it, offering to shoot fucking Velda herself, she's everywhere at once and nowhere at all, Caril Ann Fugate, she's the girl, container of multitudes, she suffered, she was there, and never was…

924 Belmont Avenue: Afterwards

Charlie would remember it   as the best week
of his life: plenty of food, bacon and eggs
every morning,   Caril there as his good little
wife,   together each and every minute
of the day   playing gin rummy, watching
Abbott and Costello   on Channel 10,
reading comic books, cutting out   paper dolls,
taking long   showers together, running naked
through the house, humping   like monkeys
in the Bartletts' big bed,   and every once
in a while there was a knock   at the door,
Caril sending them away, finally posting   a note:
Stay a way Every Body is sick with The Flue
and he would think often   of this time
later, in the penitentiary,   near the end,
think of how things   might have been different
if they could have been   the last two people
on earth,   Adam and Eve in their own
private garden   of orgasms, TV   and shotguns

Unbroken

He was a gentleman, she told herself—
refused to take her virginity even in their
weeklong vacation at the Bartletts' home,
would only put it in an inch, less,
then out again, turn her over and slide it
up her bottom, sometimes five or six
times a day in those days with her mother
and sister in the ice-shingled
outhouse, stepfather in the frozen
barn, and she wondered in that week
about words, words like *love* and *sex*
and *dead,* especially *dead,* imagined herself
stiffening next to Mother and Betty Jean
in the outhouse, stiffening as Charlie's cock
stiffens, again and again, a small corpse
pushing up into her, a part of him dead, dead
yet not cruel, not insistent: saving her,
leaving her, thank God, intact, unbroken.

Victim: August Meyer

I was afraid of him   because he was dead,
Caril would say, later   but Charlie wasn't:
easy enough to blast   the old man (80
if he was a goddamn day)   to Kingdom Come,
August Meyer, a farmer Charlie   had hunted
jackrabbits with, to take   his face off
with a squeeze of the shotgun's   trigger,
drag the carcass   to the outhouse, leave it
there, hell! Caril carried   the old man's hat
I was afraid of him   because he was dead,
she would say, later   but Charlie had
a fine time trying on   Mr. Meyer's clothes,
taking socks   gloves a new jacket
and then some Jell-O he found   in the icebox
I was afraid, she would say,   and Charlie
put his arms around her in Meyer's   coat, now his,
caressed her, put his tongue   into her little
mouth, felt his cock   getting hard, whispered
Don't be scared, dead people   don't talk
and they stood there a long time   saying nothing

Victim: Carol King

Her father's death slants to her
at odd moments, like this moment,
at her desk, algebra to be ploughed
through (never her favorite, but she
makes A's in it, in everything),
her mind wandering to choir practice
tomorrow, cheerleading again
in spring, time sliding through
her fingers now, in senior year:
and the future without Daddy, well,
that's Bob, she guesses, sweet reliable
Bob who works in the grocery store,
glasses and flannel shirt Bob,
though part of her, a small part,
but a part, might dream of a wilder man,
someone not satisfied with life as
ordained for them, marriage / house /
children / church, someone slinky
in leather, a man on a motorcycle
from a place no one in Lincoln has ever
heard of, but it's just schoolgirl
fantasy, she knows, diligently working
her quadratic equations, just movie images,
things that will never, can never
happen, and her father slips through
her mind again: God, how simple
life once was, how she misses him, so

that when Bob calls, invites her
for a ride in his truck, she says yes
instantly, anything to carry her mind
from sadness, from anxiety, from
senior-year jitters, anyway she knows
she'll marry Bob, knows they'll be happy
together in the way grown-ups in Lincoln
say they're happy, and it's all right,
really, it is, and these are her thoughts
on the evening of January the 27th, 1958,
around seven, an hour before night cold,
the storm cellar, before Starkweather.

Countdown

She won't know,
as the two figures materialize
on the road before them—a young man
with a shotgun, and a girl—that

In forty-seven minutes the young man
will be ripping a hunting knife
through her vagina,

Or that in forty-three minutes
he'll be pulling the pants down
from her dead body,

Or that in thirty-eight minutes
he'll place the shotgun behind her head
and burst her brain like crushing an egg,

Or that in thirty-seven minutes
he'll order her to walk down
the steps of the storm cellar,

Or that in thirty-five minutes
she'll stand in the Nebraska night
unable to move for terror or breathe,

Or that in thirty-four minutes
she'll watch him shove her fiancé Bob
down the steps and explode six shots
into the back of his skull,

Or that in twenty-eight minutes
he'll march both of them
across the frozen ground, shotgun
at their backs,

Or that in twenty-five minutes
he'll order them both out
of the truck, the girl holding
the gun on them as they move,

Or that in twenty-two minutes
he'll demand that they pull over here,
stop right here, while the girl tells them
they damn well better do it,

Or that in sixteen minutes
the shotgun will be aimed at Bob's neck
while the girl rifles through his wallet
and extracts four dollars,

Or that in twelve minutes
the young man will declare *You just do
what I tell you and you won't get hurt,*

Or that in four minutes
Bob will ask *Don't you drive
a Ford? Black? '49?*

Or that in two minutes
he'll turn the truck around
to give those kids a lift to town,

Or that in one minute
he'll look at her and say, *We should
pick 'em up, I think I know that guy,*

Or that in one second
two figures will materialize
on the road before them, a young man
with a shotgun, and a girl….

To the Point

In the storm cellar Charlie wanted to rape Carol King's skullshattered corpse but *it was cold* and he *couldn't get to the point,* and what do we do with this image, Starkweather over her body, a living girl a minute or two before, standing there with his dick in his hand, tugging at it, humiliation mounting, finally bringing out the knife, tearing it into her naked crotch again and again, where do we file this, in what cosmic Hall of Records, what category, what database, where do we put this so that it remains as it must under its necessary umbrella heading: *Human*?

At the Wards' House

the longer   it goes the more Charlie
   comes to feel   disembodied,
            evanescent
as if he wore wings   as if he were air
   itself, or   light: a door in the
   wealthiest   neighborhood in
            Lincoln
   opens to him without   a word of
            protest,
   he   and Caril sit down   in a
            living room
   full of soft pretty things   they hold
   guns on the lady   and her maid
            while
Charlie demands waffles   and gets
            them,
   with faster   service than any greasy
            spoon
   in the world   and it really is   a
            movie
   now, this,   everything—*The*
            Desperate
   Hours, Suddenly,   candy-ass
            homes
   burst into by   mad-dog killers,
            only
   this one, baby,   won't end with

the cool guys   getting blasted,
            cops
  rushing in: he'll lay waste
            in ways
  even Bogart   and Sinatra can't,
            won't,
  don't dare   to, tying them
            down
in dark rooms   upstairs while
            Caril
keeps watch, shoving   the knife
            into each
  of them twenty   times, thirty,
            wet
  sounds, gagged cries,   his
destiny and theirs   filling him
            with bright
  humming   lightglow, his heart
            bursting
like summer   sunshine, hotter
            than Hiroshima,
            fiercer!

Caril's Job

After the killings it's Caril's job
to pour perfume over the beds
and bodies, to mask the odors
of blood, of shit and piss,
and it works, a little, for a while,
making a smell she'll remember
the rest of her life: sweetsour, sickly,
like meat that's gone bad, maybe just
barely edible still, if you're willing to risk it.

January 28, 1958: Night

Double-locked. Deserted.
Bars shut. Whores home.
Streets silent: only old papers
rustling in breeze, only lone
cop cars sliding through darkness.

Children staring at ceilings.
Wives glancing through
windows. Husbands sitting up
in bed, fingers
stolidly on triggers.

Lincoln, Nebraska,
ten thousand sentinels
on night duty,
waiting for the graveyard shift to end.

Night Ride

Near Seward Nebraska on Highway 34
late dark Charlie loses control of the Wards'
Packard swerves from the road nearly kills
them both exhaustion he says turnpike
trance yet they must keep going eat up
asphalt miles and he tells Caril
to suck on his cock while he drives
to keep him awake and she does and he
feels the future narrowing down to just this
the night Caril's lips and somewhere
soon not yet but soon the sign he knows
he'll see planted smack in the middle
of the road the one he can't pass
or run down the one that reads DEAD END

Climax: Caril

Later she'll learn his name,
Merle Collison, learn
that he was a traveling salesman,
but in the bluecold winter's day
she knows nothing as Charlie blasts
through the driver's window into
the man's sleeping form, the man
who might be her father because
almost any man, after all, could be
her father, as blood and meat
chunks spatter inside the car,
as they burst into the vehicle
and Charlie shoves the lumpen
carcass onto the floorboards,
and as Caril sees what Charlie
doesn't, the cop car growing
in the rear view mirror, something
within her suddenly reconnects,
awakens, and, breathless,
heart smashing in her chest,
she lurches from the car, waves
wildly toward the cop as Charlie
guns the vehicle into overdrive,
bluesmoke streaming off
the roadway, and by the time
the cop is out of his car
she's shaking, hysterical,

pointing, screaming *Charlie, that's*
Charlie, Charlie Starkweather!
and as the cop, wide-eyed, radios
for backup she collapses
forever into ten thousand
splintered shards of herself,
utterly unbodied, and healed.

Climax: Charlie

One hundred miles an hour
pure power downtown
Douglas lights flashing
guns smashing James Dean
movie scene Bogart blastoff
to brightwhite eternity
terminal velocity so long
motherfuckers gotta go
cocksuckers need to catch
a flight don't forget to write
skyhigh dead dry goodbye
goodbye the end hack to
black roll credits glass
shatters blood spatters can't
see *Oh God don't kill me!*

Three

Charlie's Visits

in his dream he's surrounded   by indiangrass
taller than his head, millions   of spears of it
nearly blue under the blue   sky, the seedheads
gently susurrating   in the warm breeze,
and he wanders naked   through groves
of dogwoods, firs, bushes of   coralberry,
chokeberry, clove currant: kingfishers glide
overhead, cranes and cormorants,   and he
feels such peace, such   simple joy
that he'll remember this place   always,
visit it sleeping   with Caril
at the Bartletts', their dead   bodies freezing
in the outhouse in back,   Velda's shoved
headfirst halfway down   the hole,
find it again   at the Wards' after sinking
his knife deep into   the women's backs
and guts, amazed   at how long it takes
Lillian Fencl to   finally fucking *die*,
dream it once more   in the 8 x 12 cell where
his whole life seems to   transform to
memories   of dreams, and as they
strap him down   in the chair
he'll feel   for a final time, yes

indiangrass stroking   his skin

Self-Defense

Robert Colvert came at him—
he should have been judged

Marion Bartlett came at him—
a hero Charlie thought

Velda Bartlett came at him—
as good as Robert Mitchum

August Meyer came at him—
as goddamn John Wayne

Bob Jensen came at him—
holding them off against

Carol King came at him—
all odds every one of them

Lauer Ward came at him—
doing just what a man must do

Merle Collison came at him—
to survive in this filthy fallen world

Sinatra's Father

Near the end, Guy stands in the courthouse
hall, introducing himself to everyone as *Charlie
Starkweather's dad,* asking the warden to let him
have snippets of his son's hair, autographs
to sell: paternal pride, at least in the celebrity:
like being the father of the President,

he thinks, or Mickey Mantle's, or Sinatra's!

Insanity Defense

Guy and Helen were careful
at the trial, circumspect
to the press. What mattered,
they said, was that Charlie
never done nothing crazy
to them, it was just that he
didn't use good judgment—
and that it was really Caril Ann
who goaded him on, pressed him
forward into the vortex
of his future. *She seemed to have
a hold on him,* they said, that's
what they saw, so they asked
that no one call their son *crazy*—
and they would huddle together
outside the courthouse, hoping
against hope to push *insanity*
far from the family name, praying
against prayer to hold Charlie
among the normal, the
everyday: to keep him, whole.

The Small Animals of Nature

on the stand during Caril's trial   Charlie was asked
            if he wanted his glasses: *No sir,*
he said *there ain't nobody in here   I want to see*

            a good line, and   he smiles now,
      remembering it,   staring up at the naked
bulb which never goes dark   which will glow
      steadily even   after Charlie Starkweather
                        goes dark

and he's thinking now   about Heaven, thinks
      how once his idea of it   was like a dream
he'd had, he and Caril together   car swerving
            bullets crashing   shotgun blazing
                  in firefilled   darkness

            but now that's   gone, now
      in its place   is a green meadow, an
open pasture surrounded   by cottonwoods
      air cool   sun bright   sound of a river
            nearby   whippoorwills   loons

and he stands alone, arms   outstretched
            squirrels   hawks   rabbits all
scurrying   gliding   hopping toward him,
            all the small animals   of nature,
      and this would be   joy, communion:

eternity with soft   dumb creatures,
a world free   of the people he doesn't
want to see   which is   *Christ* all of them

Metaphor

A journalist will report
that later, in his cell, calmly
smoking, reflecting on his life,
Charlie said that he'd
had trouble, yeah, but that
he couldn't, honestly, see
where any of it was *his fault:*
others started up with him,
got in his way, he was just
defending himself. *Because
of them,* he said, *I'm here.*

He flicked the ash
of his cigarette away then,
and, inspired to metaphor,
summed up his life, Caril's,
the life of the world:
*If you pull the chain on a
toilet,* he said, *you can't
blame it for flushing.*

Portal

When the shotgun   broke apart
Lauer Ward—   or maybe it was
Merle Collison—   could have been
    Meyer, maybe,   or Colvert—
    there was   a moment when
    the guy, not   yet dropping,
    stood there   as if suspended
        between two   worlds
    and Charlie could see   clear
    through   him, like looking
    through   a portal to another
    dimension, and   he dove into
    this opening   headfirst, flying
like Superman through   the hole
    which became, as   he passed,
    a flaming   halo attached coolly
        to his   head, and when
he was   through it he floated high
above everything, all   the wreckage
    of the world, and   he was
washed clean by   fire, as glittering
    and priceless as   diamond,
    just as   hard, as   deathless.

Blank

On death row   he draws, he paints:
sketches of Caril   with the .22 in her lap,
himself with a cigarette   and windbreaker,
face thoughtful, angelic—   and a painting,
large-scale, of men   in bloody combat,
arms flailing,   mouths howling,
hundreds of them, their pain   created /
controlled by Starkweather, by Charlie Starkweather!

The picture is his   masterwork, his joy,
and he rushes to finish before   the deadline,
almost does,   but misses: when they come
for him near midnight the bodies   are complete,
the blood,   the wet wounds, the   gaping red
holes and chunk-shredded   flesh, but
the faces   all the faces   are empty,
eyeless, soulless, undone, blank—   and later,

after Charlie is just fried meat   for grubs,
a guard will remember   that canvas, shake
his head, say, *It was too bad.   It wasn't bad...*

June 25, 1959: One Last Minute

the stranger he wrote   near the end
to his mother   in a poem   *asks no greater glory*
till life   *is through*   *than to spend*
one last minute   *in wilderness*
and he had   that minute   (though less
than a minute)   at the end   just past
midnight   walking shackled from
prison hospital to   death chamber   100 yards
gray walls   beside him   gray guard towers   above
faceless men   around him   gray pavement
beneath   (avoiding cracks saving   mother's back)
but there   to his left   sheeted with light
was grass   palegray   nearly white
in the fluorescent   sheen   smooth
as a buzzcut   yet growing   sprouting
bursting the innards   of the earth
and he pictured   himself   diving into
it   rolling in   it   tearing out
clumps shouting   in joy   inhaling
them   eating   them   opening
arms to   night sky to   moon to
Nebraska wind   *one last minute*
in wilderness   and he felt love
for everyone then   everything   for Mother for
Caril for   black-capped chickadees and
love he felt   such love   love
as he'd never felt   love   O Love!

Inmate 1427

She would put it behind her, Caril thought,
when the trial began, confident she would go free.

She would put it behind her when she was given
life in the Nebraska State Reformatory for Women.

She would put it behind her during months
of solitary confinement, forbidden to speak or smile.

She would put it behind her with her studies
in prison, high school diploma, nurse training.

She would put it behind her on group visits to town,
bowling, swimming with the other girls at the Y.

She would put it behind her on parole in 1976,
walking in free air for the first time in seventeen years.

She would put it behind her in Lansing, Michigan:
a good job at a hospital there, helping the sick.

She would put it behind her someday, when she
no longer said *Caril with an i* to looks and whispers.

She would put it behind her, get married, have
children, which she didn't do, said finally she couldn't.

She would put it behind her, yes, in the darkness
of three o'clock in the morning she would know when

She would put it behind her—when there was a stone
in the cemetery with the words *Caril Ann Fugate,*

She would put it behind her then, that's when
she would put it behind her, and not then, even then.

Behind a Little Door

Caril keeps Charlie *behind a little door:*
never opens it, though maybe occasionally,
on a solitary, rainswept night, she'll
glance in, just for a moment:

and with Charlie hidden there, so is
everything else that happened:
Mom, Marion, Betty Jean and the rest of them,
hazy in memory now, as if she'd been

drugged, or hypnotized, and who knows,
maybe she was. Anyway, it—he—
sits there, in her mind, lurks there,
the door's edge sharp as a straight razor,

slicing herself off from herself, hiding
her beginning from her end, and she doesn't
open it even if she hears him screaming
back there, wailing, even if he howls to her

how lonely he is in this rain, how lost.

Collector's Item

Sometimes, in a bookstore,
she passes the True Crime section
and sees her name, her
fourteen-year-old face
emblazoned on the cover
of a lurid-looking paperback.

Once—just once—she'll pull
such a book down, scrawl
her autograph across its title page,
knowing it will soon be destroyed
as damaged goods, just as she
is damaged goods, destroyed.

Some Other

Forty years later Caril
still dreams sometimes
of Betty Ann, grown-up
now, with their mother's
eyes: she'll see her
on the street, white
blouse, '50s hairdo,
know instantly who
she is, feel tears flood
her cheeks as she
rushes forward to embrace
her, cry, *I did love you,*
I did, but when she
touches her little sister
her body seems to hold
only liquid, blood
or water, like a huge
plastic sack sloshing
softly, and Betty Ann
ignores her, keeps moving
toward a young man
standing there at the end
of the street, a man
with red hair and a red
windbreaker, far off
yet looming, a man
Caril knows that she
once knew, sometime,
somewhere,
in some other dream.

Caril Dream

One night, deep winter frost icing grass and stones around me, I find myself on an unfamiliar hilltop. There, nude, blue in hard moonlight, is Caril, fourteen, scratching at soil with her fingernails, digging small holes from which she extracts bits of dirty white bone, skull pieces, shattered chunks of spine. Leaning down to her I see she's shivering, crying, and between shallow hiccupped breaths she says to herself that she must *put them together again, hold them close, keep them warm.* She's an age my students are, an age a daughter of mine might have been. I drop down to help her, to scrabble in the frozen earth with her, thinking that maybe together we can really do this, mend them, her, us, and as I reach to touch her hand, to tell her, teacherly, fatherly, how it will all be all right now, how everything will be all right, the bright beams of headlights sweep suddenly over us and she whispers *Oh God, oh my God*, widestaring back over her blue shoulder at the '49 Ford sliding up before us, its chrome grill gigantic, invincible. *No,* she breathes as the vehicle's motor stops, *No* as the door unlatches and creaks open, as the silhouette steps out holding the silhouette of a shotgun in its hands. Utterly black, utterly silent, stockstill, the figure looms over her, over us in the slicing white glare, in no hurry, waiting, biding its time, while the words *No please, please no* drop slowly from Caril's lips, as soundless as my own heart's hot need.

About the Author

Christopher Conlon's poems, stories, and articles have appeared in such diverse publications as *America Magazine, Poet Lore, The Long Story, Filmfax, Dark Discoveries,* and *Poets & Writers.* He is the author of three previous books of poems *(Gilbert and Garbo in Love, The Weeping Time,* and *Mary Falls: Requiem for Mrs. Surratt)* as well as a novel, *Midnight on Mourn Street,* which he recently adapted for the stage.

As an editor his credits include *He Is Legend: An Anthology Celebrating Richard Matheson, Poe's Lighthouse,* and *The Twilight Zone Scripts of Jerry Sohl.* A former Peace Corps Volunteer, Conlon holds an M.A. in American Literature from the University of Maryland.

Visit him online at http://christopherconlon.com.

www.ingramcontent.com/pod-product-compliance
Lightning Source LLC
Chambersburg PA
CBHW071419040426
42445CB00012BA/1214